Also by Linda Porter Harrison

Torn Between 2 Brothas

Think Like a Man
and here's a thought...Start Acting Like a Man
The 25 mistakes men make that prevent them
from finding and keeping true love

Stuck on Stupid
or
Stuck in Stupid

The 25 mistakes women make that prevent
them from attracting and keeping real love

LINDA PORTER HARRISON

authorHOUSE®

AuthorHouse™
1663 Liberty Drive
Bloomington, IN 47403
www.authorhouse.com
Phone: 1-800-839-8640

Published by AuthorHouse 2/08   /2012

ISBN: 978-1-4685-4446-6 (sc)
ISBN: 978-1-4685-4447-3 (e)

This book is dedicated to
"My Sister Dear"

Valerie Jean Wright

Mistakes

#1 "I don't love me." The poor self-esteem syndrome.

#2 "I don't need a man."

#3 Domestication.

#4 Submissiveness…understanding your role.

#5 Being argumentative…not knowing
when to simply shut-up.

#6 Sharing too much information
with family and friends.

#7 If a man says that he's not interested in having
a serious relationship with you…BELIEVE IT!

#8 Delivery is everything.

#9 "He better fix his own plate!"
Why the little things matter.

#10 Publicly degrading your man.

#11 Punishing every guy that comes
along because of Joe.

#12 Just because you're attractive and successful
doesn't make you wife material.

#13 Generational curses. Just because your mother
and grandmother did it…doesn't make it right.

#14 Engaging in negative conversations about your husband or ex in front of the children.

#15 Not allowing your children to see their father because you are still angry about the break up.

#16 Never telling or showing him appreciation.

#17 Not supporting his goals.

#18 Letting your girlfriends determine who you should date.

#19 S.E.X. The assignment.

#20 Touch him just because.

#21 Learn to take care of you.

#22 Ask for what you want, need and desire.

#23 Get a hobby! No man wants to be up under you 24/7 and neither should you.

#24 Give him time to unwind.

#25 Stop being the "other" woman.

Stuck on Stupid:

You are wallowing in an unhealthy relationship, even though you recognize that the relationship isn't going anywhere. Then one day you wake up and decide to "unstick" yourself, brush yourself off, learn the lesson/s and move on.

Stuck in Stupid:

You have been dating the same guy for ten plus years and he still doesn't know where the relationship is heading and he isn't ready to fully commit. You have convinced yourself that he will wake up one day and drop to one knee and say, "Please marry me," or, you think he's going to leave his wife and three kids, marry you and live a faithful, honest life. You have passed up several good, single men because you know that he will come around soon. Year after year you sit around and wait…and wait…and wait. <u>Stuck!</u>

Introduction

I have been pondering whether or not to write a relationship book for women for quite some time. After the release of my first novel *Torn Between 2 Brothas* and my first relationship book *Think Like A Man*, I received numerous e-mails and phone calls from women asking that I write a relationship book for them. Initially, I was taken aback because I never saw myself as a relationship guru. The irony is that I've always been the girlfriend that everyone comes to when it comes to relationships. I don't think that it is because I have had the best relationships when it comes to men. Believe me; I have had a few that I care not to remember. I must admit, I kissed a few frogs before I found my Prince Charming. However, I do think that it is because I have always been optimistic and objective when it comes to love. Even when I have been in the midst of a tumultuous relationship, I have always been able to find my center, recognize my stupidity, and if not in that moment…very soon afterwards, get out of my circumstance. Afterwards, I brush myself off, evaluate the lesson learned and move on (something many women have trouble doing). Also, I try not to punish the next man that enters my life for the mistakes the previous guy made (huge mistake). For the last ten plus years, I have been paying close attention to the behavior of women and trying desperately to get a grip on why we continue to behave so stupidly when it comes to men. Is it that we just don't know? Or is it that we do know, but we choose to stay stuck in/on stupid? You'll have to answer these questions for yourself. Nevertheless, I hope that by the end of this book you will have gained some insight about your behavior and begin to make the necessary adjustments in your life to allow you to experience REAL love.

Blessings,

Linda

Mistake #1

"I don't love me." The poor
self-esteem syndrome.

She walked into my office and I immediately noticed that she wasn't her usual, bubbly self. Her whole being seemed drenched in sadness. I asked her what was wrong and she began to cry a soft, solemn cry as she explained her "situation." She has been dating the same guy for 12 years and he has yet to pop the question. She loves him. She wants to be married. She wants a baby, but she knows that he doesn't feel for her what she feels for him. And yet she stays and accepts his treatment. Each day she hopes that he'll wake up and change his mind. He'll realize that she's "the one."

So, I ask, "How do you feel about you?"

She says in a matter of fact tone, "I believe I am a queen and I should be treated as such."

I quickly reply, "Then why have you chosen to stay in a relationship with a man for 12 years who clearly doesn't love you?"

Silence.

And then she says, "Because I don't believe that I can do any better."

"Why?" I ask.

Silence again. I lean forward and say with a stern tone, "Tell me the truth. Why don't you think you can do better?"

"Because I'm fat and ugly," she says lowering her eyes.

"Who told you that?" I ask.

"Everyone! I've been hearing it all of my life since I was a kid." She says.

I reply, "Okay. Let me get this straight. While you were growing up, people called you nasty names and now you're in your thirties and you can't get those voices out of your head? You truly believe that you are fat and ugly?"

"Yes." She replies while nodding her head.

I wanted to grab her and shake some sense into her, but I restrained my frustration. I realized that I had heard this story a million times from countless women. Each story came in a slightly different package, but at the core of each package was a woman steeped in poor self-esteem.

What's so incredibly sad is that the majority of these women would tell you that they truly love themselves… yet their daily actions say just the opposite.

You may be one of these women and your poor self-esteem resulted from one or more of the following:

1. You did not have a positive relationship with your father or other men.
2. You have never had anyone tell you that you are worthy.
3. You have been rejected and abused by some man that you truly cared for.
4. You are overweight.
5. You are lonely.
6. You are unhappy with your life.
7. You are divorced.
8. You dropped out of high school.

9. You have red hair.
10. You have wide hips.
11. You don't have hips.

I could go on and on, but I am sure that you are getting the picture.

Whatever your reasons are for having poor self-worth… get over it! Today is a new day and you need to start loving you.

You will never attract true love until you can truly love and honor you. The truth of the matter is that men can spot a woman like you a thousand miles away. It's as if someone has written on your forehead, "I don't love me. Please come and take advantage of me."

At what point will you take control of your life? Are you in a worthless relationship? End it today. Don't allow someone to use you as their doormat. Are you overweight? Well, stop eating so much and start exercising. Are you still mad about your divorce? Get over it! He's not the only man on this planet. Are you drowning in debt? Cut up those credit cards and stop spending.

I know what you're saying, "Linda, you just don't understand. It's hard."

I do understand and yes it is hard to break an unhealthy habit, but it can be done. People do it every day. Just get off of your behind and do it. Stop waiting around for someone or something to make your life worthwhile.

You have to create the life you want. All of your wants

and desires are available to you if you would just put forth some focus and fortitude.

You are 38 years-old, single and miserable. Why? Figure it out. Take having a man out of the equation. What brings you joy? What are your dreams? What things do you need to work on? Are you selfish? Are you materialistic? Do you have the spirit of jealousy?

When you can be happy with you in your own space… then you are truly whole. Only then can someone walk into your life and share your happiness.

Be all that you can be by yourself. Work on believing that you are truly a gift from God and that you deserve the best. Then start creating the ultimate life. Whatever has happened in the past…is over.

As my Grandma Jaine would say, "If God meant for you to live in the past, he would have put some eyes on the back of your head."

It's a new day. Start loving you.

Mistake #2

"I don't need a man."

I laugh every time I hear a woman make this statement because it is usually coming from a woman that's doing everything in her power to get a man.

First of all, let's refrain from saying, "I don't need a man." You don't need a toilet, but it sure is nice to have one. No man in his right mind wants to hear this statement and most men have a desire to be needed. Not in terms of needing him to breathe or walk, but in terms of companionship. Men need to feel appreciated.

So, when you boast that you don't need a man, you are actually sending out a clear message to men that you do not need them.

Why then would a man want you in his life? When you are constantly reminding him that you don't need him.

You cannot say in one breath, "Lord, why can't I find a good man?" And then in the next breath say, "Shoot, I don't need a man. I can do bad all by myself."

It's a complete contradiction.

The statement itself is very powerful and I really don't think that women truly understand this.

We get what we say. In other words, the words that spew from your lips become prophecy. Words have authority.

If you are constantly saying, "I don't need a man!" Guess what? You'll always be without one.

Mistake #3

Domestication.

If you're a woman reading this book and you do not know how to cook or take care of a home…it's a damn shame! I said it for all of the individuals in your life that are afraid to tell you. Who are you women that do not know how to cook? You can't make cornbread unless it comes from a box. You don't know how to keep a home. You are dressed to the nine when you leave for work every day, but your home looks like a pigsty.

No man wants a woman that can't cook. I know that some of you are saying that your man cooks and that's fine. However, every now and again he is going to want a fried bologna sandwich. You don't have to be a gourmet chef. But can he get a grilled cheese sandwich once in a while? Even if your man does most of the cooking, he will appreciate the effort.

Now, on to those of you who keep filthy homes. No man wants a woman that cannot keep a clean home. If you simply do not want to clean your home then you need to hire a maid service. The way you keep your home is a pure reflection of your life. Never thought about it, huh? Look around your home. Is it cluttered? Unorganized? Is it neat? Tranquil? Now, think about your life. I'm sure you'll be surprised.

There used to be a time when women were trained by their mothers and grandmothers on how to take care of a home. In the midst of women becoming more independent we have lost this central and vital piece.

Women are the nurturers…the caregivers. We are the first teachers for our children. Now, I'm not saying men shouldn't be a part of this process…they should. I am saying that women typically teach their children how to care for themselves, but not anymore. We now have generations of women who don't know a thing about domestication, but want a man…and eventually a family.

Typically, when a man is searching for a mate he is looking for specific qualities. He wants to know that you can run a successful home and teach his future children. Sure, it may sound a bit old-fashioned, but it's so very true.

As women we have got to reclaim some basic skills. It doesn't mean going back in time, but rather acknowledging and utilizing those attributes that fostered successful marriages and families.

Visit your local library and check out a few cookbooks. Try your hand at making something simple and go from there. Go through your home and straighten up. Get rid of unnecessary items.

Make your home a true reflection of you.

When he shows up…he'll take notice.

Mistake #4

Submissiveness…
understanding your role.

What is it about the word submissive that sends women into defense mode? Is it the word itself or what many of you believe the word to be? I believe that most women automatically assume that the word means that you have to comply with everything your husband commands. This couldn't be further from the truth. I also believe that many have misconstrued the biblical meaning and have tried to use it for their own gain.

I would like to address wives. If you are married the word submissive should not make you cringe and want to pull out the boxing gloves. Your husband is your head of household...period. This doesn't mean that you do not have a say in the decisions being made in your home. You should be consulted on all major issues. However, it does mean that at the end of the day the responsibility of the family rests on his shoulders.

And before any of you start screaming about the fact that you make more money than he does, etc. I'm not talking about money. Yet many of you are under the guise that money determines his status in the home or how you choose to respect and honor him. This in itself is wrong. I realize that there are some men out there that have a problem with their spouses making more money than they do. They need to grow up. At the end of the day, if you are bringing in fifty thousand and he is bringing in forty thousand, that's ninety thousand dollars coming into the household. Enough said.

Women have been taught to be independent. As a result, we have a very difficult time relinquishing power over to our mate. It frightens us. We don't like being told "No" or that we shouldn't do something. Better yet, when he tells us that he'll take care of "it" we immediately start thinking of how we can intervene to insure that "it" is done right. Even in some of the simplest situations we don't know how to step back and let our mate take the lead.

It's a pattern that's difficult to break, but it can be done.

Here's an example: You tell your husband that you want to get a new washer and dryer. The set that you want is $3000. Your husband says that you can get the washer and dryer, but to wait until the end of the month so that you guys can pay cash for it. You angrily storm out of the room because you wanted the set now...not three weeks from now (even though the set you have is old...it still works). So, you decide to bypass his directive and you have the set delivered the next day. When your husband arrives home from work he is livid. You tell your husband that you put it on your credit card, so it shouldn't be a big deal.

Believe me, this scenario is a daily problem for thousands of couples. I have heard hundreds of women make comments like, "He can't tell me what to do with my money. I go to work every day just like he does!"

Ladies, you are missing the point. It's not about your money or his money...technically the money belongs to the both of you. It's about you not willing to listen to your husband. Waiting three more weeks for a washer and dryer isn't going to kill you. Now, it changes if the machines don't work. Then you need a new set immediately.

However, many of you operate in this mode of disrespect and expect to get loving results in return. It won't work and eventually you'll drive him away.

Here's a helpful piece of advice. If you are married to someone that is responsible, loving and respectful... allow him to lead. Good men consider their women when making decisions. Good men do everything in their power to protect their women from harm.

Learn how to honor your husband or mate in small situations, so that it will be easy to do when faced with something monumental.

Let him be the man that he is designed to be. Then, you go out and enjoy being a woman for once in your life and not have the worry of trying to be a super woman.

Mistake #5

Being argumentative…not knowing
when to simply shut-up.

I am chuckling as I write this mistake because I used to be so guilty of this flaw. I had to have the last word. My favorite line was, "I need clarity because we (meaning him) are not clear on this issue!"

I would go on and on until I felt as if my partner finally "got it."

Then I married Scott and all of that changed. My husband does not believe in arguing. He believes that you can have a disagreement and still be respectful of one another, but if things started to get loud and out control then everyone needed to take a break.

I was not accustomed to this. I was used to getting my point across and battling it out. I was going to have the last word…period.

So, when Scott and I had our first disagreement I did my usual spill. I went on and on for nearly twenty minutes. Scott looked at me and asked, "Do you want me to simply listen or do you want me to respond?" I thought to myself, "Are you a fool? Do you think I'm telling you all of this relative information for nothing?"

I replied, "I want you to respond!"

He said, "Ok, but not right now." Scott got up from his chair and walked away.

I screamed, "What do you mean later? I $%#@&*^% need clarity!"

Scott replied, "Later," and continued walking down the hallway.

Boy let me tell you, I was hotter than Fourth of July fish grease. What the jack did he mean later? I sat there pouting for awhile and then I went about my business.

The next day, I was ready to give it to him and again he simply said, "Later babe."

Now I am really pissed because this man has had more than twenty-four hours to get his thoughts together. So, I thought, "Okay, you can play this game if you want to, but when you do get ready to talk to me you are really going to get a beat down!"

The next day, the exact same thing.

By now I am starting to forget why we were disagreeing in the first place.

Day three. Scott says that he's ready to talk.

"Linda, I love you. And because I love you I never want to speak to you when I'm angry. When people are angry they have a tendency to say things that are hurtful…things that they can't take back. That's why it's important to take a day or two to really think things through before you respond. So, when I say to you let's discuss it later it's for the both of us."

What I have found is that after a few days you are not angry anymore, and you're able to have a calm and respectful discussion.

To this day, Scott and I are able to have the most difficult conversations in a manner that makes us both feel as if we've been heard.

All without arguing.

**Here's an extra caveat for those women who like to get up in a man's face when arguing. Cease immediately from this behavior. When you approach a man as if you are a man or hit a man, you run the risk of being dealt with like a man. I am in no way advocating that a man should hit a woman. This is an absolute no-no. However, women need to understand that they should not confront a man aggressively or put their hands on their mate. There are many men that will not simply turn their cheek if you cross these boundaries.

It is never okay for either sex to approach the other in a violent, uncontrolled manner.

Mistake #6

Sharing too much information
with family and friends
(they will never forget).

When women are involved in a relationship and something goes wrong, their first instinct is to pick up the phone and call a family member or friend. We do this because we want confirmation. Especially confirmation that is in agreement with us.

For example:

You have been married to Eric for five years. The last two years have been the most difficult. The two of you can't stop fighting over the finances and Eric just blew your entire savings on a new business venture that went sour. Not to mention, you caught him looking at porn and sending salacious e-mails to some woman on the Internet. You are livid and you need to vent.

So, what do you do? First, you call your mom and she immediately says, "Oh baby, come home for a few days. Your dad and I would love to have you home."

You hang up the phone and dial your sisterfriends on three-way.

"Girrrrrl, if I were you I'd put his behind out...today! You are smart and attractive. You can get someone else!"

Now, everyone is in your business. By the end of the day your mom has told your dad and your dad has told your brother and your sisterfriends have discussed it with their sisterfriends and now the entire city is burning up about you and Eric. All because you couldn't keep your business in your home.

A few days go by and you and Eric decide that you are going

to seek counseling and work through your issues. Things are back on track and you and Eric are inseparable.

Well...not quite. See, you involved your family and friends in your business and they are still pissed at Eric and they are not going to let you forget it. As soon as Eric does something else they are going to give you a detailed account of everything that this man has done to you and they will not hesitate to tell Eric about himself.

It will be as they say in the South, "A hot mess!"

I truly understand the need to vent and wanting to have a second opinion. However, discussing too many of your intimate matters with outsiders can create nothing but havoc in your home.

At the end of the day, you and your husband are the only two individuals that can fix your problems.

Unless you are seeking counseling from a professional, keep your business just that...YOUR BUSINESS.

Stop telling everyone what goes on in your home between you and your man and start talking to your man. You never know, the person you're sharing too much information with may use it to try and get your man.

True communication is one of the keys to a successful relationship and it starts at home.

Mistake #7

If a man says that he's not interested
in having a serious relationship
with you…BELIEVE IT!

You've gone out on a few dates with Paul and you've had a great time. He is handsome, smart and quite witty. You want to pursue a relationship. However, he has said in each of his conversations with you that he only wants to be friends.

Paul is very clear about the fact that he is focusing his time and energy on his career right now. He says that he can't afford the distractions of a relationship.

You hear him, but you don't **hear** him. You want Paul and you're going to do whatever it takes to get him. So, you start your quest of "getting Paul." You start sleeping with him, cooking for him and being at his beck and call.

A month goes by and you show up at his condo unannounced. "Oh, I was just in the neighborhood," you say.

Paul shakes his head in disbelief and explains to you again that he only wants to be friends and that he prefers that you call before stopping by his place.

You apologize and assure him that it will never happen again while you gingerly slip out of your slip dress and whip it on him. You pull out all of your tricks because you are going to convince him that you are "the one."

After your heated session, Paul tells you that he needs to get some rest and you gather your things and leave.

The next day, you show up at Paul's job with flowers. Paul is having lunch with one of his female co-workers. You quickly approach Paul and try to kiss him on the lips but he turns his head and you end up kissing his cheek. He starts to introduce you, but before he can get anything out you exclaim, "Hi, I'm Paul's girlfriend!"

Paul quickly takes you by the hand, walks you outside, and lets you have it. He tells you that he has explained to you a thousand times that he isn't interested in being in a relationship with you and that from your recent behavior he can't see himself being friends with you either.

You are pissed! Here you are doing everything under the sun to prove to Paul that you care about him and want to be with him.

What do you get in return? Nothing.

Listen up women! If a man tells you that he is not interested in pursuing a serious relationship with you...believe it! No amount of sex, food or booze is going to change his mind.

If you happen to meet a man that you're interested in and he doesn't feel the same way...just move on. If you don't, you will suffer. You cannot make someone love you.

When a man wants you, he will pursue you!

Mistake #8

Delivery is everything.

We are natural communicators. As I mentioned earlier, women love to talk. However, when it comes to talking to our men we tend to fall short. We simply do not know how to talk to our men.

I can't tell you the number of times I have been at a gathering and I hear women talking to their mates as if they are children. These women show no respect or regard for their partner's position or feelings.

Things like, "Shut up!" or "You are such an idiot!"

Men do not respond well to confrontation or disrespect. Do either of the aforementioned and you are bound to get the silent treatment or better yet, a disappearing act.

There is this tone that most women have (you know that I am telling the truth) and it balances on being extremely curt or just plain mean. It's the same tone you use when you are disciplining your children, but you tend to forget that your mate isn't your child. He's a grown man.

How many times have men mentioned to you that you do not know how to talk to them? Or, have told you that you need to work on your mouth?

Try this experiment. Ask your beau to bring to your attention each time that you speak to him in a disrespectful manner. He has to point it out immediately when it's happening so that you can actually hear what he is hearing. I think that most women would be amazed at how often they talk down to their men.

Let's say for instance your husband didn't put the trash out last night and your garbage wasn't picked up this morning. Instead of going ballistic on him and saying, "Why can't you ever remember to do anything around here? You are such a lazy bum! I have to do everything!"

Try saying, "Babe, you forgot to put the trash out today. Will you please make an effort to remember next time? Or, "Would you like for me to remind you the night before?"

See, two totally different approaches. It seems like something quite miniscule in the big scheme of things, huh? Believe me, it is one of the biggest complaints I hear from men.

Talk to your man with a kind and considerate tone. You'll be amazed at the response you get.

Remember…delivery is everything.

Mistake #9

"He better fix his own plate."
Why the little things matter.

When Scott and I started dating, I noticed that he ate out almost every day of the week. I am not a big fan of eating out every day. I prefer to cook my own meals so that I know exactly what I am getting. Since I fixed my lunch every day, I asked Scott if he wanted me to start fixing his. He said, "Sure." Thus began this interesting journey.

The first lunch that I prepared for Scott was honey turkey breast on whole wheat with a little bit of mayo and mustard. I put his lettuce and tomatoes in separate containers along with two pieces of fruit, yogurt and a bag of chips.

When Scott took his lunch break several of his female co-workers made the following comments:

"Humph, this ain't gonna last. Just give it a few weeks and you'll be on your own!"

"Shoot, my husband better fix his own lunch or stop at Mickey D's."

Now, fast forward to our first family reunion together. All of the men were sitting around talking, playing cards, etc. I asked Scott what did he want to eat and proceeded to fix his plate and bring it to him. When I gave him his plate the entire table went silent. You would have thought the Almighty One had just walked up.

"Wow man, she fixes your plate? I can't get my wife to fix me a peanut butter sandwich!" All of the men started giving each other high-fives in agreement. "You got yourself a good one."

Whenever I think about either of these situations I always

laugh because I cannot fathom not doing something as small as fixing my husband's lunch or plate. I love him. Why would these things ever be an issue for me?

How can you say that you love someone, but you are not willing to do the small things? Think about it. If you won't do the small things then there is no way that you will be there when he really needs you.

I can see some of you rolling your eyes right now and having big attitude. "Why can't he fix my plate?" You are absolutely right. Your partner should be willing to do the same for you. However, we are not focusing on what men should or shouldn't do, but dealing with our baggage right now.

The next time that you go to a family gathering, pay close attention to how many women actually fix their significant other's plate. I dare you to count.

Although I focused on the lunch and plate scenarios, they are just examples. There could be other small areas in your relationship that you are neglecting. Stop here for a moment and think of some small things that you can do for your mate to show him how much you care.

Little things go a long way.

Mistake #10

Publicly degrading your man.

I am not going to spend a great deal of time on this mistake.

When you publicly degrade your man, you are slowly chipping away at his self-esteem and self-worth. Believe it or not, your man really does want to be the apple of your eye. When you decide to display his faults and inabilities in front of others, you are also making a statement to others that you do not respect him.

"Girl, I wish our yard looked like yours. My husband is useless around the house."

"Mom, I wish Tim were more like Dad. I mean, he never spends any time with the children. I don't think he's a very good father."

"Oh Susan, your husband looks so good to be 40. Look at my blubber butt husband. He's gained fifty pounds since we married. I can't stand it!"

"Please don't give that to my husband. He can't fix a thing. He is no handyman."

Need I say more?

Never embarrass or degrade your husband in public. It is disrespectful and truly unkind.

Mistake #11

Punishing every guy that comes along because of Joe.

You dated Joe for three years and then everything went downhill. He decided he wasn't happy with the relationship and broke things off. You cried every day for six months. You were drowning in sorrow. A year and a half has gone by and you can't seem to get him out of your mind, but Joe has moved on. He is married and they are expecting their first child.

You are devastated. Why didn't he marry you? You wanted to have his babies. What does this woman have that you don't have? You are mad at the entire universe. "No man is ever going to hurt me again…ever!" This becomes your daily mantra.

Then you meet Max. Max is a wonderful guy. He works full-time for an architectural firm and has his own landscaping business on the side. He's funny and he absolutely adores you. Every weekend you guys have done something together. You've never had anyone send you flowers just because or call you in the middle of the day just to say they're thinking of you. He's a good guy.

Now, winter has rolled around and it's football season. Max tells you that he likes to watch the Sunday games with his boys and that he'll be going out of town for a few of the games.

You immediately wail into him. "What do you mean spend time with your boys? Oh, you can't watch football with me? Why do you need to go out of town to a game when it's being shown on television? You must be going out of town to see some slut! I knew you weren't &*%#! You men are all the same!"

Wow! All of this drama just because he wants to enjoy a few football games with his boys?

Max of course is stunned. He doesn't know where all of this anger is coming from. Then it dawns on him. He remembers all of the things you shared with him concerning your past relationship. It clicks.

Max sits you down and explains that he isn't your ex-boyfriend and he has no intention of hurting you. He also tells you that in order for you guys to continue to grow as a couple you are going to have to trust him and fully let go of your past.

You continue yelling at Max and say that you can never trust another man and that all men lie. Max tells you that you are going to miss out on a good man because you can't get over a bad one.

You don't listen and you tell Max that it's over and that he can just go hang with his boys.

Another year goes by and you run into Max at a restaurant with an attractive woman. Max speaks and then says, "This is my fiancée, Wendy."

You are stunned and you angrily walk away. How could he do this to me? Men are dogs!

Nooooooooo! It's not the men. It's you! Do you hear me? It's you!

You were hurt and for whatever reasons you've not been

able to close that chapter of your life. Now, every guy that comes your way will be punished because of Joe.

Everyone has had their heart broken at least once in their lifetime. It's a part of life. Most of us cry for a while and then slowly pick ourselves back up and move on with life. We realize that Joe is only one guy, not every guy.

If you do not grasp this concept, you will grow old and gray all alone.

There are a lot of good, available men looking for good women.

Don't miss out on love because you can't get over "the one" that didn't love you in return.

Mistake #12

Just because you are attractive
and successful doesn't make
you wife material.

There, I said it! It needed to be said. I realize that this mistake is going to burn a lot of butts. Oh well, I haven't bitten my tongue thus far.

What is with you women that believe that just because you are attractive and smart, it automatically qualifies you as being a "good catch?" And the only thing that you have to do is show up, have sex and the ring is on the way.

You have focused so much of your energy on being cute and successful that you have never paid attention to those core essentials that go into making you a whole person. You've never taken the time to focus on those key elements that a woman must possess in order to be a complete woman. It's those elements that men really look for in a mate.

Yes, a man wants someone attractive and successful. He also wants someone that can be his partner and eventually the mother of his children. You will never fit the bill if you don't take some time and work on being unselfish, less materialistic and developing some domestic skills.

I applaud those of you that have gotten a formal education and are notably employed. I am always proud to see a woman that has taken this path and made her own way. I am such a woman.

I wanted to attend college and establish myself in my fields of study. However, at some point I realized that I wanted to be more than just attractive, smart and successful. I wanted to be a good person…inside and out. So, I started working on the essence of Linda and believe me that went far deeper than just being attractive, smart and successful.

There seems to be a plethora of women walking around with this elitist attitude. What's so incredibly funny is that when you hear men say things like, "Yeah, she's fine and she has a good job, but she's soooo selfish and self-centered. I can kick it with her, but that's it." This statement is made nearly every day inside of your neighborhood barbershop.

I remember someone telling me that her girlfriend was a really good woman and that she just couldn't understand why she couldn't keep a man. She went on to say that she was cute, intelligent and had a great job.

I turned towards her and politely said, "You're her girlfriend. Of course you think she's a good woman. But you've never dated her. There's a huge difference."

She felt like so many of you reading this right now. You're walking around believing that you are the ultimate catch just because you possess the previously mentioned qualities. Yet, you haven't worked on the "essence" of you.

So, what happens? You meet a man and he is thoroughly impressed with your package until you open your mouth and he listens to how messed up you really are.

Looks and smarts may attract him, but they won't keep him. Make sure that your outer beauty matches up with your inner beauty.

A complete package attracts and keeps her man.

Mistake #13

Generational curses. Just because
your mother or grandmother
did it…doesn't make it right.

One of my girlfriends got married and her husband said that he wanted them to combine their checking accounts. Her immediate response was, "Oh no! My mother and grandmother told me to never put all of my money with my husband's because you never know what might happen. Always keep yourself something hidden on the side."

Now, most women have heard this particular statement throughout their entire lives. When you really think about the statement, it reeks in deceit and mistrust.

So, my response was, "Are you telling me that you married someone that you don't trust? If you have to hide money from your husband, you shouldn't have married him. Do not bring your mother's or your grandmother's mess into your home."

A lot of times we allow our mother's habits and beliefs to become a part of our own. Even though we may feel uncomfortable in our spirit doing what is suggested.

Maybe your grandmother stayed in an unfulfilled marriage because of the children and now she is a bitter, old woman. Do not let her opinion of men drive your belief.

I am not saying to disregard all advice from your mother or grandmother, but when the advice is motivated by contempt, anger and mistrust…leave it. Whatever worked or didn't work for the women in your family shouldn't have any bearing on your relationship.

Create your own system based on the relationship that you have with your man and not someone else's.

Mistake #14

Engaging in negative conversations
about your husband or ex in
front of the children.

I walked outside of the library (where I work) to take a break. I wanted to enjoy a moment in the summer breeze before starting my afternoon program. I sat on the brick wall, which was a few feet away from a group of teen girls that were engaged in a heated discussion about men. They didn't notice me. These girls attended the middle school that sits directly across from the branch and frequented the library daily. They ranged in age from probably eleven to thirteen years of age. I sat in shock as I listened to the following conversation:

Girl #1: "Shit, my mom says that you can't trust a man as far as you can see him."

Girl #2: "I know that's right. My mama says that all men are dogs."

Girl #3: "Yeah, and all men lie."

Girl #4: My mama says that my daddy has never paid a penny in child support and that's why he ain't worth the ground we walk on."

Girl #1: "I know that's right. My mom says that's why I need to work hard and get a good job so that I don't have to depend on a man for nothing!"

They all proceeded to laugh and give each other high-fives. I shook my head in disgust and slowly walked back into the library. Wow! Where did these innocent girls get these despicable images? Their mothers.

How incredibly sad. At such innocent and fragile ages these girls have contempt towards men.

I could have stopped the conversation and told them that what their mothers said about men was not accurate and that not all men lie or cheat. This of course would have immediately caused some friction. I would've been saying the opposite of what had been implanted in their minds.

Young women trust and get the majority of their information from their mothers. Saying anything contrary to that belief would not have gone over well.

Women, please stop talking negatively about your mate or ex in front of your children. Even though I used the example of the teen girls, it could have easily been a group of teen boys saying, "Yeah, my mom says that my dad is worthless and I'll probably be just like him."

You chose to have children by this man. Good, bad or indifferent. No one forced your hand or held a gun to your head. The relationship isn't working or didn't work. Move on.

If you do not have anything good to say then simply keep your mouth closed. Do not make your kids dislike him just because you do.

Mistake #15

Not allowing your children to see their father because you are still angry about the break up.

Ladies, ladies, ladies. Why do you use your children as weapons? It's wrong. It's petty, and in the end it only destroys the children.

If it didn't work between you and your ex it doesn't stop him from being dad.

So many of you use excuses like: "Well, he doesn't pay child support," or, "He's re-married and I do not like his new wife."

At the end of the day, none of these excuses matter. If he isn't paying child support, take him to court. If he has re-married, good. He's not your problem anymore and as long as his wife isn't abusing your children...chill.

Learn this simple lesson:

<u>A father will make an impression on his children whether he is in the home or outside of the home</u>.

At some point children grow up and they will form their own opinion about their father. You do not need to play a negative role in this process.

Always...always tell your children to respect their father. Even if you think he is unworthy of respect.

Children need fathers. Don't prevent your children from having a positive relationship with their father just because you're still hurting.

Regardless of what you may feel about him, he's still their dad.

Mistake #16

Never telling or showing
him appreciation.

If you do not tell your mate that you appreciate and love him, he will seek this validation elsewhere.

Why is it so hard to tell the person that you supposedly love that you actually love them?

When was the last time that you told your husband how much you appreciate all that he does for you and your family? When was the last time that you simply said, "Honey, I love you."

That long huh? Not good.

Men need to know that they are appreciated and not just once a year on Father's Day. Outside of sex, this is huge for a man.

Showing that you appreciate your mate goes beyond just saying it. What's your husband's favorite meal? Cook it tonight. Does your husband enjoy fishing? Surprise him by packing up his gear and telling him to enjoy an entire Saturday at the lake. Remember that sexy teddy that he likes so much? Wear it tonight…just because.

Validate your man at home, so he won't seek it when he leaves.

Mistake #17

Not supporting his goals.

Believe it or not, most **good** men want to give you the world. They want you to wake up each day with a smile. They want you to feel secure and protected.

The same set of desires hold true for men. They too, want to wake up with a smile. They want to feel secure and protected by you, but in a different manner.

He needs to know that you have his back and that you support his dreams.

Ask any man what he desires most from his mate outside of love and sex, and he will unequivocally say, "I need her to support me."

Here lies the issue:

Most women do not know how to show support without coming across too bossy and most men do not know how to articulate what they need. So, it puts us all in a quandary.

Start by asking your mate the following questions:

1. What are your goals? For yourself? For our family?
2. What do you need from me in order to accomplish these goals?

Pay close attention to his answers and respond accordingly. Remember, this isn't about you. So, do not try to interject your opinions. Your man faces many challenges in this world. The one assurance that he needs is that you are in his corner.

Mistake #18

Letting your girlfriends determine
who you should date.

Why is it that single, unhappy women have all of the advice in the world when it comes to men? Yet, they can't seem to get a man...yet alone keep a man. Things that make you say, "Hmmm," huh?

I am always amazed at how freely these women spew information or opinions.

"Girl, he's a school teacher...ugh, they don't make any money."

"He drives an American made car! Oh, he is cheap...he definitely can't afford you."

"He asked you to go to the gym with him? What? Is he calling you fat?"

"Girl, he is too short."

"Did you see his shoes?"

"Let's Google him."

"He doesn't have a six-pack."

"He's 35-years old and has never been married? He's gay!"

Do you see where I am going here? All of the questions and comments are meant to make you second-guess your choice when you may have a really good guy on your hands. Have you ever thought that because your girlfriends are miserable, they want to keep you miserable too? Think about it.

If you meet a man that you like (the operative word here is **you**), that's all that matters. At the end of the day, the relationship is between you and your man...not you, your man and your girlfriends.

So what? He drives a Ford Taurus. He has a car. So what? He works on a garbage truck. He makes more money than a whole lotta folk walking around here and you can clean him up when he gets home. So what? He's skinny. You can cook him up some home cooked meals and plump him up a little.

And,while you and your skinny, Ford Taurus driving, garbage truck working man are cruising the Caribbean for a winter getaway...your single, know it all girlfriends will be at home wishing that they had a good man like yours.

Mistake #19

S.E.X. The assignment.

Okay, this is an assignment rather than a discussion about a particular mistake. It will only become a mistake if you do not follow through with the assignment.

I want you to find a quiet moment with your mate and ask him a few questions. Now, before you ask him these questions please put your ego aside. He may say something that hurts your feelings or embarrasses you, but he is not trying to hurt you nor be malicious…especially if he loves you.

Listen to his responses and do not respond immediately. You will have your chance to give him feedback.

Before you ask these questions tell your mate that you love him and that you want to have the ultimate sex life with him. Assure him that you will not take any of his statements personally, but as constructive sharing.

This is a very sensitive task, so don't engage in this conversation when you are angry or frustrated with your mate.

Questions:

1. Do you enjoy having sex with me?
2. If yes, why? If no, why not?
3. On a scale of 1-10, where would you rate our sex life?
4. What would make it a 10?
5. What things do you like for me to do sexually?
6. Are there some things that you would prefer I didn't do?

7. Do you have a sex fantasy that you would like to explore?
8. What is favorite time of day to have sex? Why?
9. Is there a particular way that you'd like to see me dress when it comes to lingerie?
10. Do you think I am shy or inhibited when it comes to sex?
11. Would you like for me to initiate sex more?

After he has answered each question, it's now time for you to open up and have a heart-to-heart discussion.

If your mate says some things that hurt your feelings... shake it off. This is not the time for you to become overly emotional. Rather, take the approach that this dialogue will bring the two of you closer. Reiterate that you appreciate his honesty.

Now, tell your mate (calmly) how you feel about your sex life. Share with him any inhibitions you have when it comes to sex and why.

For instance:

Do you feel uncomfortable getting on top? Why? Are you ashamed of your body?

Do you dislike oral sex? Why? Is it because you're not quite sure you're doing it right?

Ask your mate to show you how he wants things done. He is your best teacher.

This is an opportunity for you and your mate to really

connect. The reason why so many couples seek sexual satisfaction outside of their home is because they have never taken the time to really talk about their own sex life. NOW IS YOUR TIME!

When all is said and done (especially if the two of you are honest), you'll end up being each other's "best ever."

Mistake #20

Touch him just because.

Men are just like women when it comes to showing affection…they need it.

I am not talking about being lewd or lascivious in public, but rather something as simple as holding hands or giving each other a peck before parting ways.

Sometimes, it's you patting him on his behind when he walks past you or kissing him on the nap of his neck. These little signs of love show him that you care for him and that he still turns you on.

So, the next time you see your man, walk up to him and lay one on him. Do it slow and make it intense.

He'll probably laugh and ask, "What's gotten into you?"

Your reply should simply be, "Oh, I wanted to put something on your mind."

Believe me, he'll be thinking about it all day.

Touch your man just because…not just when you want some.

Mistake #21

Learn to take care of you.

I must admit, this is by far one of the hardest lessons I've had to learn. As a natural born giver and nurturer, I have a tendency to over extend myself. This leads to me feeling stressed, exhausted and incredibly frustrated. I didn't know the art of simply saying, "No."

Thank God, I no longer have this problem.

I have learned that when I am spiritually sound and physically fit, I am a very happy person. I feel good about me and that transfers into being good to others. However, when I am running around taking care of others and neglecting me...I am ill. Mentally and physically.

So now, I take care of Linda...period.

I didn't come to this conclusion on my own. As a matter of fact, it was after the birth of my son and my husband actually suggested it to me.

Our son attended daycare during the week. Since I was off on Fridays, I would keep him home with me. Well, one day I was complaining about how tired I was and never having any time for myself. My husband looked at me and said, "You cannot be a good wife and mother if you don't take care of yourself. Make Friday your "me" day."

At first I was a little apprehensive being a new mom and all, but I remembered hearing other women telling me to make sure that I took time out for me. So, I did it! Fridays became my official "me" day and I have never looked back.

I wake up on Friday mornings and go for my run and

then enjoy a cup of my favorite coffee. Afterwards, I may lounge a bit and then I am off! I may go out and get a full-body massage and facial. Or, I may visit a new restaurant or vineyard. Who knows? It's my day…interruption free, and I love it.

When my family arrives home I am a renewed woman.

I know that many of you are saying, "Linda, I don't have enough time." Yes, you do. You may not have an entire day, but you have a few hours that you can set aside each week just for you.

Take care of yourself, so that you can take care of the important things in life and enjoy doing it.

Remember that you matter.

So, don't wait another day. Make that appointment at the spa and enjoy, enjoy, enjoy!

Mistake #22

Ask for what you want, need, and desire.

If you only take away one bit of information from this book…let it be this.

In order to create the ultimate relationship, you have to learn how to communicate. There is simply no way around this rule. As I stated earlier in the book, women are natural communicators. We talk all of the time with our family and friends, but shut down when it comes to our men (except when we're angry).

We are quick to tell our girlfriends when we need help or when we are feeling unappreciated, but run into a brick wall when we need to tell our mates the same thing.

Why is it so hard to tell our husbands what we need?

I can hear women across America screaming:

"He should know what my needs are. We've been married for ten years!"

"Why do I have to tell him that I need help? Can't he see that I'm exhausted?"

"He should know what turns me on."

I could go on and on, but the reality is that men simply do not operate the way we operate. <u>If you do not **say it**… he will not **get it**</u>.

I pride myself in keeping a clean home. It's just the way I was raised and it's in my blood. I have to have a clean, organized living space or I feel out of sorts. Well, when I gave birth to our son it added a dozen plus chores to my list.

As I mentioned earlier, I'm quite anal when it comes to the upkeep of my home. For those of you that have children, you know firsthand how exhausting the first few months can be. I was in a coma...literally. I have never in my life experienced this type of fatigue. My little pumpkin was on the breast like clockwork. If his feeding was at 12 p.m., he started squirming at 11:59 a.m.

Like so many women, I felt as if my husband should have noticed that I needed assistance. Didn't he see that I was comatose? No, he didn't. Why? Because I never said anything. I never complained. Then one day, all of the s%#@ hit the fan. I went off.

"What's wrong with you?" I yelled. "Don't you see how exhausted I am? Are you freaking blind? I NEED HELP!"

My husband looked at me the way he always does when I behave like a mad woman and calmly said, "Babe, what is it that you need? All you have to do is ask."

That pissed me off even more. "Why do I have to ask?" I screamed.

Scott explained that I'd never voiced that I needed anything; therefore, he thought things were fine. He said that I was just my usual, happy self. So, how could he know? He went on to say that since I shared with him what I needed, he was more than willing to oblige. In that particular moment…I got it and I have never forgotten it.

If you want something from a man, you better open your mouth and ask for it.

Instead of walking around pissed off about what he didn't do or what he didn't pay attention to…just ask him to do it. Believe me, you both will be happier in the long run.

Men are not wired like us. God didn't make them that way (Thank God!). So, instead of trying to make him more like you, except that he is different and learn to communicate in a way where he will get it.

Start today by opening up to your mate. Tell him what you want, need and desire from him. If he truly loves you, he'll go out of his way to make it happen.

Mistake #23

Get a hobby! No man wants to be up under you 24/7 and neither should you.

I can remember this as if it were yesterday. I was having a "Girl's Day Out" with a few associates and one of the women was in a new relationship and quite excited about her newfound love. We were also thrilled about her new romance. However, throughout the entire outing she kept complaining that she missed her new beau. Even though she had only been away from him a few hours.

After making the same statement over and over again, I'd had enough. I blurted out, "What is wrong with you? We have only been out for a little while."

She replied, "Oh, I just can't stand being away from him. We spend all of our time together."

We all started laughing because this sounded so ridiculous coming out of a thirty-five year olds mouth. At this point, we tried to explain to her that it was healthy for them to have separate activities, but she wasn't listening.

One of the women reminded her that baseball season was just a week away and that she was sure that he would want to watch some of the games with his boys.

"Oh no, I am positive that we will be watching all of the games together," she firmly stated.

Again we all laughed and shook our heads. Then someone said, "When you told him that you were hanging out with us today, what did he say?"

She replied, "He said to have a great time and that he was going golfing with his buddies."

We tried again to convince her that this was good for the relationship, but we could see that she was in her own world.

Needless to say, baseball season rolled around and what did he say to her? "Babe, I'm going to watch the game with my boys."

Eventually, he also told her that he enjoyed their time together, but he thought she needed to have some interests outside of him. She was devastated.

When she called me, I simply said, "So, what's your new hobby?"

Listen up ladies:

Once you become a couple you don't stop having individual interests or likes.

For instance, if there is a "Law & Order" or "Godfather" marathon on television, I am glued to the flat screen and happy as a log. My husband will watch one episode with me and that's it.

Now if it's football season, my husband can sit in front of the television all day and not experience a moment of boredom. Give me one game and that's it for me. I simply have no desire to watch football all day long.

So, when my husband is engulfed in football with his boys it allows me time to do what I want to do. I may catch a matinee with a girlfriend or write a few chapters. Who cares? It's my time. When he gets home, we indulge in each other. He's happy...I'm happy.

It is so frustrating to see couples that don't do anything apart from one another. The husband can't go to a basketball game with his boys or the wife can't go to a concert with her girls. All because one or both partners is insecure and that insecurity is usually rooted in infidelity. So, what do these couples do? They smother each other in an effort to prevent future cheating. It never works.

If your mate is going to cheat and dishonor the relationship it won't matter the time of day. Cheating can take place at eight o'clock in the morning or eight o'clock at night. Smothering your husband or mate won't keep him faithful.

You should have a few things that you enjoy that don't include your man. It makes for a healthy friendship and ultimately, a healthy marriage.

Get a hobby. TODAY!

Mistake #24

Give him time to unwind.

I am sure that every woman reading this book has heard this before. It is really a simple rule of thumb. Men need time to unwind when they come home from a hard day's work.

This means that they need thirty minutes to an hour of relaxation before you really start talking to them…about anything.

Now, I understand that there may be times when you cannot afford your mate this sacred time, but under normal conditions please allow him this small block of time.

I had to learn this very thing in my own relationship. There were times when my husband would arrive home and I would immediately start telling him about my day. Keep in mind that he hadn't even taken off his shoes yet. I would go on for about an hour, none stop, and don't let it have been something that I was angry about…ohhh boy!

I can laugh about it now because I have learned how to communicate with my mate, but in the early days it was rough.

One day my husband said, "Linda, just give me a few minutes to relax and then we can talk about whatever you like." It wasn't what he said, but how he said it. There was a sense of sincerity in his voice that made me pause. Later that evening he explained that when men come home it's like they are coming to their sanctuary. It's the one place that offers peace.

So, when they come home and they're bombarded with

stuff it really makes them shut down rather than open up. The thirty minutes or more really helps them to clear their minds and prepare them for their family time.

Many of you are saying, "Linda, we don't need time to clear our minds and prepare ourselves for the family."

Yes we do…we just don't take it.

That's why I previously stated that we need to take out time to care for ourselves.

Men are different and nothing is going to change that. They need time to unwind.

So, now I make sure that my husband gets his space. When he comes home, I have his dinner cooked and I try to place the newspaper, his pajamas and his towels out for him. That way he can just relax and wind down.

Afterwards, I can talk to him about any and everything under the sun.

It sounds really simple, but thousands of women make this mistake every day.

When your mate gets home this evening, kiss him and tell him to relax uninterrupted for thirty minutes.

Believe me, he will take notice and you will immediately notice a sense of calmness take over him. Afterwards, tell him about your day. This time he'll **really** listen.

Mistake #25

Stop being the "other" woman.

I cannot tell you how many times I have witnessed single, seemingly smart, attractive women settle for married men. Year after year passes and they sit idly for him to leave his wife and children.

Every Christmas is spent with his family and every summer they enjoy a fabulous family vacation. Recently, they just purchased their dream home…but he insists that he is unhappy.

He chimes on a weekly basis that his wife isn't affectionate and that they never have sex. Yet, they have four children.

Just give him a little more time to get things in order and then he's going to divorce her.

So, you wait…and wait…and wait. Year after year goes by and you settle for every Friday at eight…at your place (because you can't be seen in public together).

Each year a piece of you slowly dies. Each year you start to question your worth. Each year you tell yourself that you must not be good enough or pretty enough.

Five years go by and he tells you that he can't do this anymore and that he's going to try and work things out with his wife. You are devastated. You scream, "I thought you loved me!"

He walks away…on to the next one.

You kick yourself for being so stupid, but even more so for

passing up all of the offers that you received from good, single men.

Men that you wouldn't give the time of day to because you were waiting for Bob to leave Mrs. Bob.

All I can say is, "You have been stuck in stupid."

Now what?

First of all, you need to ask for forgiveness because marriage is a sacred covenant between husband, wife and God.

I can hear some of you justifying your actions by saying, "Well, that's between him and his wife," or, "If his wife was doing what she was supposed to be doing he wouldn't have been at my house."

Regardless of what's going on in his household, it is between him, his wife and God…period. You are not a part of the equation.

When I meet women who settle for this role it simply makes me sad, because what you are really saying is that the God that designed this universe didn't create someone just for you. So, you'll just pick off of someone else's tree. It also screams that you don't believe that you are worthy or deserving of your own mate.

If you do not respect someone else's institution of marriage you will never experience the institution for yourself.

Ask yourself: Do I really want a man that will cheat on

his wife and kids? Will I ever be able to fully trust him if he left her for me?

Both answers should be a resounding, "NO!"

There is someone just for you. Be patient and he will find you.

In the meantime, don't settle for the scraps that a married man is throwing your way. He is never going to leave his wife and kids. Okay? And believe me; you do not want that on your conscience for the rest of your life.

If you are involved with a married man…end it today.

You are worth more. You are a gift from God and should be treated as such.

Men treat us the way we allow them to.

The day that we start respecting each other as women and valuing the institution of marriage…we'll see a paradigm shift in the way our men behave towards us.

Today is a new day. Stop cheating and start truly loving you. Then and only then will your true love appear. And guess what? He won't be wearing a wedding ring!

A HEART-2-HEART CONVERSATION

When I finished writing Think Like a Man, I decided to add a few extra mistakes at the end of the book. The added mistakes were things that I felt couldn't be overlooked or brushed under a rug.

This was also my intent for Stuck on Stupid, but my thought process took on a different path. Instead, I have decided to simply have a heart-2-heart conversation with you.

My first request is that you go somewhere quiet, where you cannot be disturbed for several minutes.

Turn off your cell phone and any other items of distraction.

Calm your mind---take a deep breath---read.

To my married sisters:

You have taken the ultimate vow between you, your husband and God. It is a serious vow. It is sacred. Do not wear the title of "Mrs." lightly, because it carries a huge responsibility.

You are the nurturer, the teacher, the organizer, the cheerleader and the comforter. Your family finds peace and rest in your arms.

Respect your husband. Assist him in areas where he is

weak and build him up through acts of kindness and loving words. Go on dates with your husband and work at maintaining the passion in your relationship. Learn to talk to your husband and allow him to be your best friend.

For those of you with children, please listen up. If you have a son...step back and allow your husband to teach him how to be a man. That's not your role. Obviously, you married your husband because you felt he was a good man. Why then would you not trust his judgment when it comes to your son? As women we have a tendency to over nurture our sons and make our daughters super independent. As a result, we have a whole society of boys that can't do anything for themselves. They can't cook, they can't clean, they can't balance a checkbook...they simply can't. Why? Because you have done everything for them. It is not healthy.

Remember that your son will eventually become someone's husband. So, teach him the same things that you would teach a daughter and then allow your husband to teach him how to be a man.

Stop making your daughters grow up so fast and allow them the opportunity to simply be girls. Why are you allowing your daughters to dress as if they are twenty-five when they are only fourteen? They are babies, not grown women. Every day I watch young girls leaving school in 4-6 inch stilettos, skirts so short you can see their underwear and enough make-up on for a stage play. What are you doing to your daughters? They will grow up soon enough. Childhood is a precious time. Let them go through the stages slowly. When you present your young girl to the world as an adult, you put her at risk of attracting unwanted and dangerous advances.

Also, don't make your daughters so independent that they don't feel comfortable asking for help. Otherwise, they will spend their lives trying to be a super woman. Teach them that are strong, but also let them know that it's ok to be vulnerable.

In the midst of all of this, remember to take care of you. Don't skip your routine medical exams and make exercise a part of your daily life. A happy wife and mother equate to a happy home.

Wake up each day and ask God to guide your footsteps. He'll always lead you in the right direction.

To my single sisters:

Why are you single? Is this by choice? If this is the case, it's okay. Do not let anyone sway you into thinking that there is something wrong with you. I am a firm believer that you can be single and happy. As a matter of fact, if you can't be single and happy you'll have a difficult time attracting real love. So, to you sisters I simply say "Keep being happy!"

Now, to those sisters who desire to be in a relationship, but can't seem to get it right.

I want you to do something that I mentioned earlier in the book. I want you to take a man completely out of the equation. Now what? Are you really happy with your life? If not, why?

I really believe that this is an important step to address because so many of you believe that having a man will complete you and make you happy. This couldn't be further from the truth.

See, you want a man to show up and be completely "on the ball," marry you and make you happy. While you just show up.

After six months of marriage you wake up and realize that you're still not happy. Listen up! It has absolutely nothing to do with having or not having a man. It's all about you.

I really need for you to get this because it is the core of why so many women are single.

No man wants the weight of your complete happiness on his shoulders. It is unrealistic to expect this from any human being.

So, I need for you to figure out why you are not happy and work on fixing it…alone.

Are you in debt? Seek the help of a financial advisor.

Are you overweight? Talk to a nutritionist and a fitness trainer.

Do you want to go to college? Visit one of the campuses in your home town.

You have the power to create the life that you want, but the first step is making sure that you're complete…**by yourself**.

Also, many of you may not want to hear this but I'm going to say it anyway. When Mr. Right comes after you (remember it is his responsibility to find you), he may not look like you. In other words, if you're Asian he may not be Asian. He may be Greek. Or if you're African-American waiting for Morris Chestnut, don't be surprised if someone that looks like Brad Pitt shows up…lol.

Seriously women, you have got to learn to keep your options open. Men do it all of the time and we need to start exercising the same right. At the end of the day, a man is a man…period. They each come with their set of issues. No one is perfect. So, instead of getting bogged down on skin color…look at the character and heart of a man.

In the meantime…work on you.

Love will come later…and believe me…you'll be ready.

THANKS

A special thanks goes out to the Las Vegas-Clark County Library District and the St. Louis Public Library District for opening their doors and pulling out the red carpet for me.

Thank you Tavis Smiley and Dr. Cornel West for granting my first nationally syndicated radio interview.

Thank you Tony and Marci Holt for your love and friendship.

Thank you Pauline McClain, Carnita Reed, Jennifer Wilson and Zenola Diggs for your encouragement and for your prayers.

Thank you Scott and Austin for making every day special. I love you both so very much!